DEVELOPING PROCESS WRITING SKILLS

Primary Writer's Workshop

by **Carol Kieczykowski**

FEARON TEACHER AIDS
A Division of Frank Schaffer Publications, Inc.

Thankfully dedicated to the children and teachers
at Westfield Village Elementary School—
especially Barbara Valdez, Mary Jo Driver, and Kathy Harper

Editor: Susan Eddy

This Fearon Teacher Aids product was formerly manufactured and distributed by American Teaching Aids, Inc., a subsidiary of Silver Burdett Ginn, and is now manufactured and distributed by Frank Schaffer Publications, Inc. FEARON, FEARON TEACHER AIDS, and the FEARON balloon logo are marks used under license from Simon & Schuster, Inc.

© Fearon Teacher Aids
A Division of Frank Schaffer Publications, Inc.
23740 Hawthorne Boulevard
Torrance, CA 90505-5927

4 5 6 7 8 9 TCS 01 00 99 98 97

Contents

Food for Thought

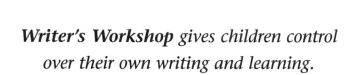

Writer's Workshop *gives children control
over their own writing and learning.*

*When children are respected as writers
and carefully led through the process,
they are freed to write, and they do it gladly
—with a sense of enthusiasm.*

Introduction

As I was putting together the manuscript for *Primary Writer's Workshop*, I could not help but reflect on how much my philosophy of writing in the primary grades has changed over the years. I was taken back to the time when I thought that first-graders could only copy class-generated stories from the chalkboard—or when writing meant little more than practicing the formation of letters. Who would ever have thought that first-graders had the ability, knowledge, and desire to be authors all along. I simply was not focused enough to see that all these children needed was the time, the opportunity, and the proper environment in which to grow as writers.

I thank Lucy Calkins and Donald Graves for their dedicated work in developing the writer's workshop concept. Their success with primary writers inspired me to attend a variety of workshops on the topic, and I soon began to thirst for more knowledge about how to free my first-graders to be the authors I knew they could be.

Several years later when I was teaching in Ohio, I had the opportunity to attend a workshop given by Regie Routman. She, too, had recognized that the writing process was a missing component in many language arts curricula. She promoted the vision of reading, writing, listening, and speaking as the necessary and inter-related components of a successful language arts program. I implemented many of Regie's suggestions and found myself instructing first-graders in a new environment that offered them many opportunities to see themselves as both readers and writers. Other teachers on my staff were beginning to notice our writing projects, and parents were providing extraordinarily positive feedback. It wasn't long before I was invited to provide inservice training for other teachers in a neighboring district.

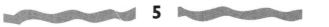

Through the years, I have modified many of the structural components of Writer's Workshop for the primary setting. Often, primary teachers become discouraged with process writing because it becomes too much of a managerial issue. They shouldn't. My training from Laurna Curran in cooperative learning at the primary level helped me find ways to alleviate this problem and to adapt higher level process writing strategies effectively for primary children. And in recent years, the work of Marie Clay and the Write Group has helped me better understand both the stages of writing and the skills that need developing along the way—which has led to more manageable, child-centered assessment.

The biggest driving force in the publishing of *Primary Writer's Workshop* has been the support I have received from the primary teachers at Westfield Village Elementary School in West Sacramento. During my three years there as a reading and language arts specialist, these teachers willingly opened their classrooms to me—allowing me to create a Writer's Workshop program that worked for them. After only a short time, we all observed boosts in self-esteem, greater enthusiasm for writing, improved reading and writing scores, and faster language development in children of all ability levels, including our ESL children. Children felt successful and in charge of their own learning.

It is my hope that *Primary Writer's Workshop* provides you with some helpful new ideas and strategies to add to your existing writing program—or that it inspires you to create a Writer's Workshop of your own. I am confident that both you and your children—*all* of them—will enjoy and profit from the experience.

C. K.

Benefits of Writer's Workshop

In the past, kindergarten and first-grade language arts programs consisted primarily of reading, phonics, and oral language development. It was not until the 1980s when the whole-language movement became popular that primary teachers began to notice that *writing* was a necessary but missing component in most language arts curricula. Once these teachers began to recognize and capitalize on the fact that young children had wonderful stories to tell by offering the proper encouragement and the right environment, their children became enthusiastic writers. Primary teachers who have incorporated daily writing into their curricula have noted the following significant benefits.

✎ Increased Self-Esteem

Since Writer's Workshop is totally individualized, all children—no matter where they are developmentally in their writing—are validated for their efforts. All children are viewed as authors with important stories to tell. What's more, children are encouraged to write about personal experiences and feelings—to "write what they know."

Writer's Workshop works especially well as a vehicle to build self-esteem for Chapter I and ESL students. Examples of their published work are provided here. All these children wrote about personal experiences and were bursting with pride when they sat in the Author's Chair to share them.

Nicole is a kindergarten student. Ben is in grade one and Karen is in grade two. Brandon, a second-grade Chapter I student, was heard to say, "The best part of Writer's Workshop was hearing everyone tell you what they liked about your writing!" He also enjoyed having one-on-one time with his teacher.

by Nicole

I SAW A MOUSE

By: Nicole
Jan. 11, 1993

Nicole

When I went to put my receipt in my backpack, I saw a mouse.
1.

I went and told my teacher and she said, "A-a-a-h!" Then she called John.
2.

The kids were all scared. They were sitting on the floor.
3.

John came in and put a poison thing where I saw the mouse.
4.

The end

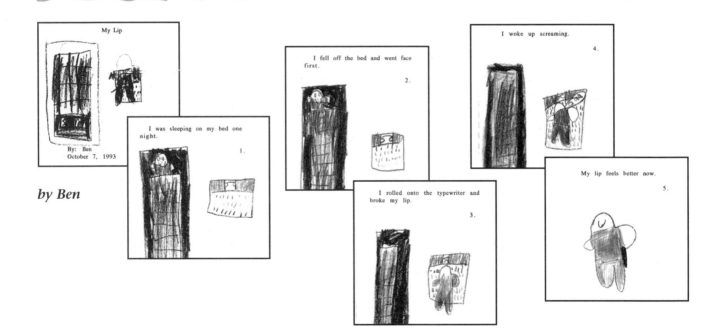

by Ben

My Lip

By: Ben
October 7, 1993

I was sleeping on my bed one night.
1.

I fell off the bed and went face first.
2.

I rolled onto the typewriter and broke my lip.
3.

I woke up screaming.
4.

My lip feels better now.
5.

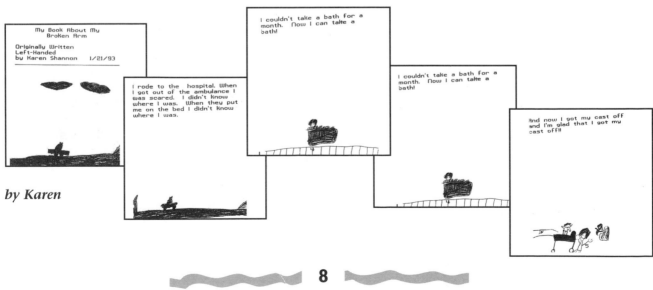

by Karen

My Book About My Broken Arm

Originally Written
Left-Handed
by Karen Shannon   1/21/93

I rode to the hospital. When I got out of the ambulance I was scared. I didn't know where I was. When they put me on the bed I didn't know where I was.

I couldn't take a bath for a month. Now I can take a bath!

I couldn't take a bath for a month. Now I can take a bath!

And now I got my cast off and I'm glad that I got my cast off!!

Student Empowerment

Children, not teachers, are taught to compliment one another with *specific* praise and are encouraged to celebrate one another's successes. They become more responsible for their own learning because they are charged with being positive critics. To do this, children must listen attentively to peer sharing, as well as to mini-lessons and writing goals taught in the classroom. Knowing what to listen for in their classmates' work helps them know what to strive for in their own.

Risk-Free Environment

Children are encouraged to write freely, using temporary or invented spelling. The emphasis is on content. Form and mechanics become secondary.

The following story was written by Bobby, a Vietnamese ESL student in a sheltered kindergarten. At the time he wrote his story, Bobby spoke little English and was very shy. He was extremely reluctant to get up in front of the class and share his work or his ideas. So it was doubly amazing when one day, Bobby asked for a turn in the Author's Chair. Proudly, in a near whisper, he shared his story about the seed. He spoke in simple sentences, but his ideas told the whole story clearly. His classmates were delighted because they were doing a unit on the carrot seed and were familiar with the planting process. Bobby received many compliments and went home on cloud nine that day! The next day, he even had the courage to read his story to the principal. Writer's Workshop often provides the environment for small miracles.

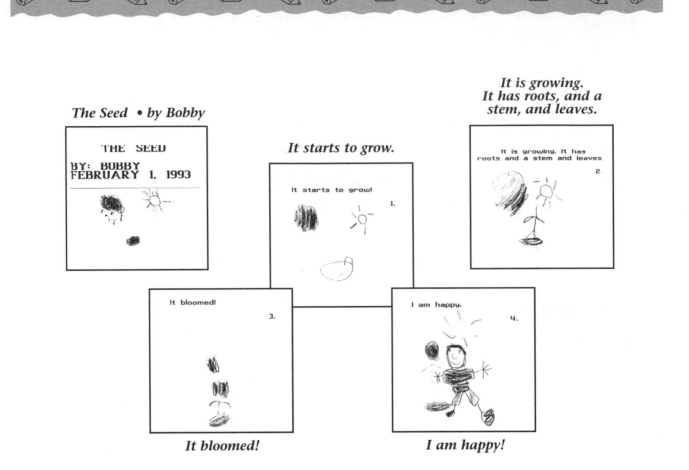

The Seed • by Bobby

THE SEED
BY: BOBBY
FEBRUARY 1, 1993

It starts to grow.

It starts to grow!
1.

It is growing.
It has roots, and a
stem, and leaves.

It is growing. It has
roots and a stem and leaves.
2.

It bloomed!
3.

It bloomed!

I am happy.
4.

I am happy!

✎ Phonemic Awareness

Phonics, as it relates to reading and writing, is given an authentic setting during Writer's Workshop. Invented spelling is phonics in action. Children's readings of their own invented spellings further reinforce the phonetic process. Primary teachers should be sure to include direct phonics instruction as part of their language arts programs so that emergent writers have the tools necessary for invented spelling. This is easy to do in a whole-language classroom. As you introduce a piece of literature, select a phonemic element to develop and help children make a class book about it. For example, you might choose *th*. You can brainstorm a list of *th* words with children and invite children to illustrate each word for the book. For a greater challenge, help children create sentences with *th* words to illustrate, such as *Thank you for the thin thimble*. Keep the little books in the classroom library to use during writing time.

✎ Increased Fluency in Reading and Writing

Early and emergent readers and writers become more fluent in classrooms where Writer's Workshop occurs because they are given opportunities to publish *their own words*. Ownership becomes the vehicle for fluency, because they witness the fact that writing is really nothing more than thoughts, observations, or conversations written down. The key, however, is that the thoughts and conversations are their own.

✎ Opportunities for Development of Oral and Written Language Conventions for Second-Language Learners

ESL students have many more opportunities to be exposed to proper conventions of language when they are part of a reading and writing classroom. They benefit from both peer and teacher conferences as well as from whole-class sharing sessions. The published books of their classmates become cherished reading material that is patterned, predictable, and supported by illustrations.

Here are three samples taken over a three-month span that show how quickly an ESL child in a second-grade writing process classroom is gaining command of the English language. Igor's first book contains very short, patterned sentences. His next book, while still patterned, includes longer sentences. Igor's third book boasts more than one sentence per page. In addition, he is beginning to use descriptive language.

All About Me

by Igor K.

Me can run on grass.

I can swim at water.

I can ride my bike.

Me can walk.

Plants

by Igor K.

You can plant apples at your house.

You can plant oranges outside.

You can plant lemons.

You can plant flowers.

Zoo

by Igor K.

I see monkeys at the zoo. They are brown. They can climb trees.

I see a lion at the zoo. He has a yellow mane.

I see bears at the zoo. Some are brown. Some are white.

I see a giraffe at the zoo. He has a long neck.

✎ Sample for Authentic Assessment

Writer's Workshop provides children, teachers, and parents with writing samples that can be collected and evaluated in such a way as to show growth over time. No fill-in-the-blanks test ever created for primary children can reflect a child's growth as a writer the way a writing portfolio can—even a portfolio kept for one or two months. Parents are thrilled to see progress, and children are excited by their growing bodies of work. And as teachers, we know that excitement, enthusiasm, and parental support are some of our best allies in the classroom. Even if authentic assessment is not used for every subject area in your classroom, you will find it works beautifully in a Writer's Workshop setting. Instructions for setting up writing folders and checklists for assessment may be found on pages 17 and 18.

Organization and Structure of Writer's Workshop

Arrange Your Classroom

Before you can begin your Writer's Workshop program, you will need to consider the physical arrangement of your classroom and the types of materials you will use. Try to create the following areas in your room:

Mini-Lesson Area

This area can simply be a carpeted area in the front or back of your room large enough for all your children. Use a signal when moving children in and out of the mini-lesson area—the 3-2-1 countdown works well. Holding up three fingers tells children to stand quietly, two fingers asks children to face the area they will be moving to, and one finger means children may move on soft feet into the designated area or back to their desks.

Peer Conferencing Area

Primary writers need separate areas away from their desks in which to share and discuss their work. You may wish to designate two corners of your room as peer conferencing corners. The steps for conferencing are as follows:

- Read and Listen
- Compliment
- Question and Suggestion
- Make It Better

Steps for Peer Conferencing

Read and Listen

 Compliment

Question and Suggestion

 Make It Better

✎ Materials Area

Primary writing materials should be labeled and organized in such a way that young writers may access them easily. Make it the children's responsibility to properly care for and return all materials. Your materials area may be as simple as a tabletop, a drawer, or a reachable shelf. You will need to supply the following:

Writing Needs ~
- blank books (premade in a variety of shapes and sizes)
- newsprint (lined or unlined, depending on grade level)
- stapler
- staple remover (aka "jaws")
- pencils
- crayons
- markers
- stamp pads
- rubber date stamp
- rubber stamps for manuscripts, such as *Author in Training* or *Rough Draft*
- file folders (children's names clearly written on each)
- manila envelopes (to hold finished work)

Publishing Needs ~
- tagboard for covers
- plastic book-binding combs
- book-binding machine
- brass fasteners
- metal rings
- hole punch (single or three-ring)
- colored pencils (for illustrations)
- computer and printer
- computer paper
- glue

✎ Folder Storage Area

Young authors need assistance in organizing their work. Once you set up a workable system, they will be able to do their own organizing—an important skill for primary children to master. You may wish to use manila file folders to hold *work in progress* and large manila envelopes to keep safe track of *completed pieces*. Store these in boxes or baskets you have placed in the materials area. An individual writing folder might look something like the one below. A sample topic sheet may be found on page 38.

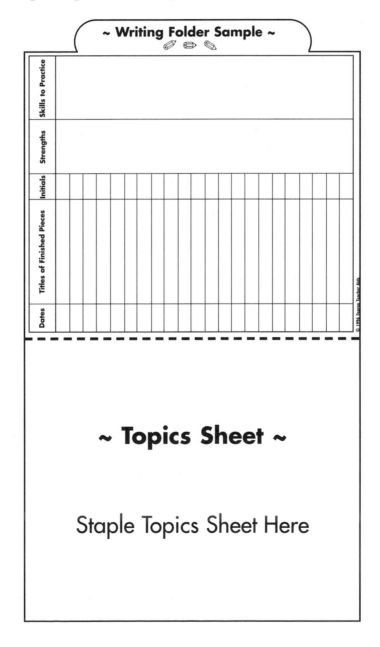

~ Writing Folder Contents ~

Dates	Titles of Finished Pieces	Initials	Strengths	Skills to Practice

✏ Whole-Class Sharing Area

All authors need an audience! Be sure to designate an area of the room that can serve as the gathering place for whole-class sharing. You may prefer a carpeted area large enough for children to gather around the author, who is seated on the Author's Chair. A director's chair, rocking chair, or tall stool makes authors feel quite important.

Arrange Your Schedule ✏ ✏ ✏

Now that you have arranged your classroom for Writer's Workshop, you will need to adjust your schedule accordingly. Most primary teachers find that the following time frames work well.

✏ Mini-Lesson: 5–10 minutes

During a mini-lesson, you may wish to do one or more of the following:

- reinforce procedures for Writer's Workshop;
- share or model some examples of quality writing;
- present one or two methods children may try to improve their overall writing, such as using more "juicy" words and more descriptive language.

✏ Writing and Conferencing: 20–25 minutes

Four stages of the writing process may be occurring during this time:

- prewriting (thinking charts, mind maps, clustering, think-pair-share, whole-class brainstorming);
- drafting (children compose rough drafts; teachers hold content or organizational conferences);
- revision (peer or teacher conferences; children revisit their work; children make changes based on feedback, such as rearranging pages, adding detail, or using more descriptive words);
- editing (individual teacher-child conferences).

✏ Group Share: 5–10 minutes

There are two possibilities for group sharing:

- Two or three children can share their work with the class.
- All children may share their work in pairs.

Introduce Writer's Workshop to the Class ✏ 🖋 ✏

Now that your classroom is arranged and your management system is in place, you are ready to introduce Writer's Workshop to your children with a series of mini-lessons.

Begin by calling children into the mini-lesson area. Ask if anyone knows what an author is. Then ask if anyone thinks that he or she is an author. Explain that in Writer's Workshop, everyone becomes an author who publishes wonderful, illustrated books to share with the class. For this to happen, however, there are some rules everyone needs to know and observe. In the beginning stages of instituting Writer's Workshop, many of your mini-lessons will deal with these **procedural issues**. Be sure you cover each of the following topics. Keep in mind that you may need to revisit these issues from time to time.

✏ Rules

Depending on the grade level you teach, your rules list may resemble this one. Consider adding rebus pictures (pictorial directions) to each item on your list.

Rules for Writer's Workshop

Speak in quiet voices.

Use quiet feet.

Conference only in
Peer Conference Corners.

Work really hard!

Put everything away
properly.

✎ Materials

Explain all resources and materials you have provided for your young authors. Demonstrate how they are to be used and cared for. Devise a way for children to let you know when materials need replacing (dried-out stamp pads) or refilling (stapler). Consider having children take responsibility for setting the dates on the date stamps and being sure the stamps are all accounted for.

✎ Folders and Envelopes

Explain to children what they will keep in their writing folders and where the folders will be kept. Show them an actual folder with contents and topics pages attached, as well as the envelopes that will be used for completed work. Primary children may enjoy decorating their folders and envelopes to make them unique and special.

Once you have carefully explained the rules and management techniques to children, they are ready for a mini-lesson on the *steps of the writing process*. For kindergartners and first-graders, consider explaining the steps in *I Can* statements such as the following. Be sure to have with you examples of how children's work *looks* at each of these stages. You may wish to post a chart outlining these steps along with rebus picture reminders. It is particularly important for Chapter I and ESL children to receive the sheltering that rebus pictures provide.

1. **I can think.** *(prewriting)*
   Show children a completed mind map or story structure.
2. **I can write.** *(drafting)*
   Show children an unedited first story draft based on the above mind map or story structure.
3. **I can share.** *(revising and editing)*
   Show children a story that has had revisions made as the result of a peer or teacher conference. Discuss how those revisions have been made.

The Writing Process

Prewriting ~ I can think.

Drafting ~ I can write.

Revising ~ I can make it better.

Editing ~ I can use my checklist.

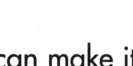

Title of My Story:
☐ I used my best handwriting.
☐ I used capital letters and periods.
☐ I drew pictures that go with my story.
☐ I practiced reading my story.
My Name_____

Publishing ~ I can select my

best work.

4. I can select my best work. *(publishing)*
Share a completed student book. It is helpful if one book is the focus for all the above presentations, so children may see the progress and the *process.*

Now you are ready for a mini-lesson that will introduce ***mind-mapping*** using thinking charts. The thinking charts included in this book are simply graphic organizers that provide children the freedom to develop their topics using graphics. You may find your first-graders using words as well—that's great! It is helpful if you model the structure and use of thinking charts or graphic organizers for children in various content areas throughout your day. Adapt the ones included in this book, use some from the many books of reproducible ones now available, or create your own.

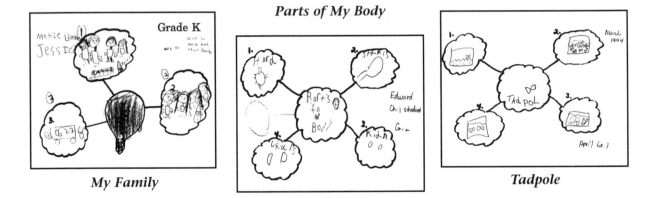

My Family

Parts of My Body

Tadpole

Other prewriting organizers may be modeled and used as well. When children use prewriting structures, their narrative story writing becomes much more developed and organized. The following story structures were completed by Chapter I students in grades K–2.

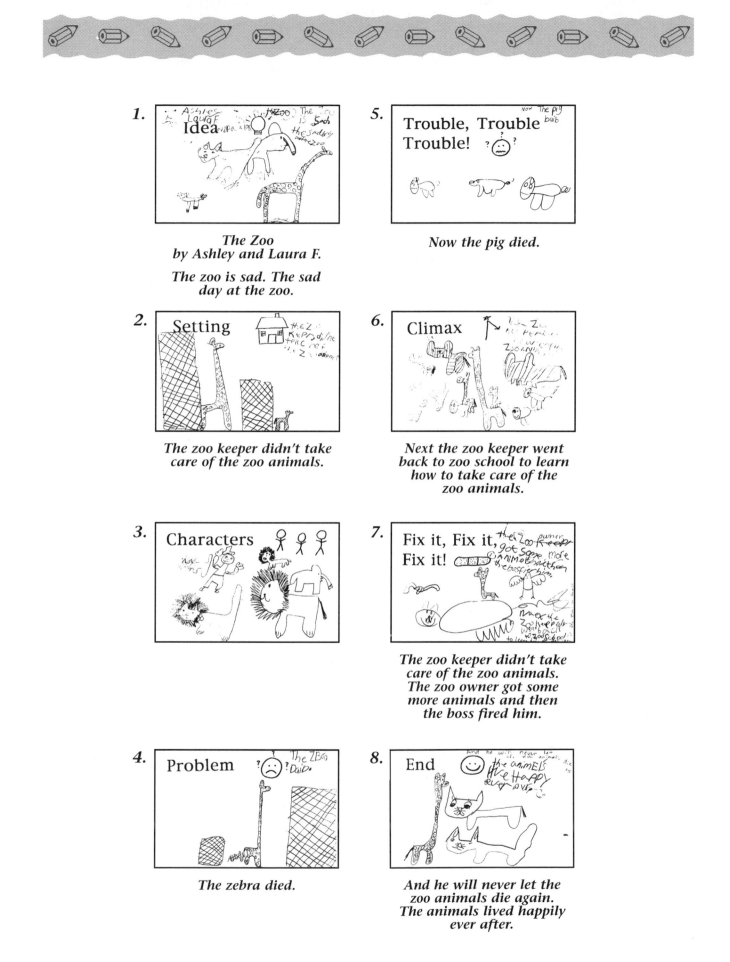

1.
Idea

The Zoo
by Ashley and Laura F.

The zoo is sad. The sad
day at the zoo.

2.
Setting

The zoo keeper didn't take
care of the zoo animals.

3.
Characters

4.
Problem

The zebra died.

5.
Trouble, Trouble
Trouble!

Now the pig died.

6.
Climax

Next the zoo keeper went
back to zoo school to learn
how to take care of the
zoo animals.

7.
Fix it, Fix it,
Fix it!

The zoo keeper didn't take
care of the zoo animals.
The zoo owner got some
more animals and then
the boss fired him.

8.
End

And he will never let the
zoo animals die again.
The animals lived happily
ever after.

1. Idea — Caroline Frank

2. Setting

3. Characters

4. Problem

5. Trouble, Trouble Trouble!

6. Climax

7. Fix it, Fix it, Fix it!

8. End

✎ See pages 27–29 for black-line masters that can be used for mind mapping.

✎ See pages 30–36 for prewriting story structures.

✎ See page 67 to read rough draft developed from the above story structure.

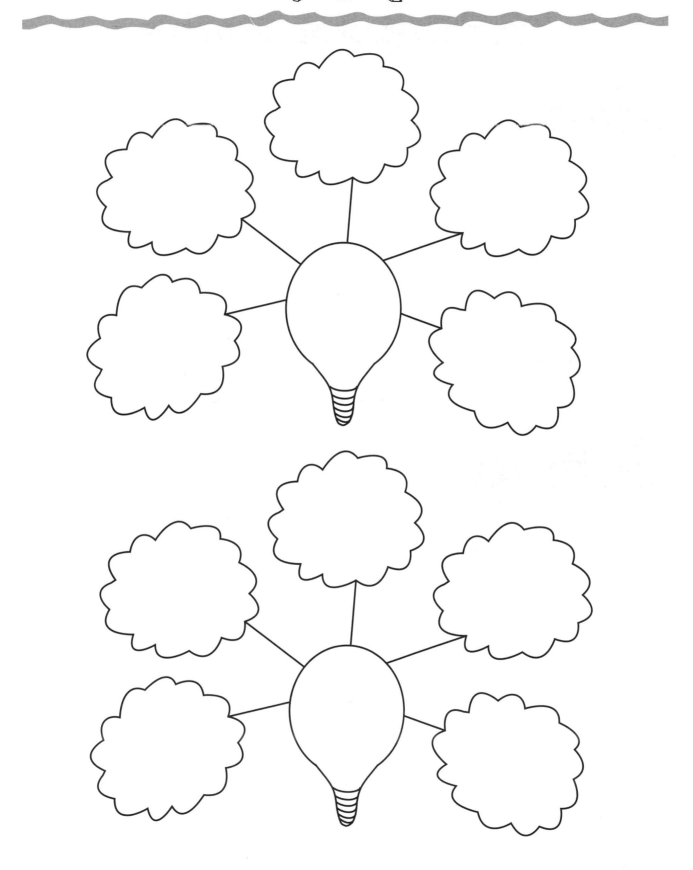

Name_____

Prewriting Story Structure
for Regular Stories

Idea

Setting

Characters

Problem

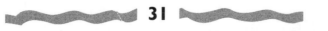

Trouble, Trouble Trouble!

Climax

Fix it, Fix it, Fix it!

End 🙂

Name_____

Prewriting Story Structure
for Fairy Tales

Good Characters

Names:

Where do they live?

How do they look?

How do they act?

- -

Bad Characters

Names:

Where do they live?

How do they look?

How do they act?

Magic

What kind is it?

How does it work?

Who owns it?

- -

Problem

What is the trouble?

Solution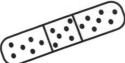

How will you fix the trouble?

- -

Reward

Who will get it?

What will it be?

Topic selection is the next area to address in a mini-lesson. You may wish to develop a Hot Topics chart with your children. As you and the children cover specific content-area material, discuss current events, take field trips, hear guest speakers, and make discoveries, add these items to the chart. The Hot Topics chart soon becomes a meaningful source of writing topic ideas readily available to all children. Be sure to supply rebus pictures, so that the chart has meaning for every child. An example follows.

Topic selection may also be facilitated by sending home the worksheet entitled *My Topics* (see page 38). Children may each fill out this sheet with the help of their families and return the sheet to school. Staple the returned topics sheets into the children's writing folders for future reference during writing conferences. If parent support is a problem, you may wish to buddy-up with children from an older grade. Older students will enjoy interviewing the children and recording their responses on topics sheets.

~ My Topics ~

Hobbies	Friends	Family

Holidays	Special Places

Favorite Activities	Pets

Happy Times	Sad Times

Children are now ready to begin writing. Invite children to write in book format—emergent readers and writers are extremely comfortable with the notion of making little books. Demonstrate how to make one by stapling some pages together on the left-hand sides (vertically or horizontally—it doesn't matter). Be sure to set limits for number of pages and number of staples! Show children where to place the title, name of the author, date, and illustrations. Discuss and model the various types of emergent writing. Children at the emergent stage may draw, scribble-write, or use isolated letters to tell their stories. If letters are used at all, they will probably be letters that appear in the children's names or that appear in environmental print, such as Stop signs or familiar logos. Be sure you validate each stage. See page 60 for some examples of emergent writing.

Encourage children to write freely on *self-selected topics* for the next three or four weeks. The emphasis should be on thoughts, ideas, and self-expression (content), not on correctness. Some examples of this type of writing follow. These particular samples are from Chapter I students in grades one and two. In all cases, the emphasis was on self-selection and on sticking to the topic. One or two items for young authors to concentrate on each day are plenty! You will see that these children remained on topic and supported their topics nicely with details on each page.

The Princess and the Prince

by Nicole

The princess was doing her hair on her bed.

Then she heard this car and she said, "Darn it!"

Then the princess was in a car and she didn't know that he was going to marry her.

And they got married.

(You may now kiss the bride.)

Weather

by Shannon

It is raining now.

It is a sunny hot day.

It is snowing.

It is fall today.

Me and My Cat

by Alex

I like to play with my cat when I am at home.

My cat goes wild in the morning and I laugh.

I pet my cat when I am at home.

My cat purrs so I pet her and I do.

My cat sleeps on my bed when it is sleepy.

My cat comes in when it rains and I dry him off so he don't catch a cold.

My cat follows me to the bus stop so I run fast.

As children are writing, you will begin holding *teacher conferences* with children who have completed their first books. Conferences are done individually, so children may comfortably share their writing with you. Papers should remain in students' hands, so they feel "in control." Ask children questions such as *How is your piece going? How do you feel about this topic? Is there anything I might help you with? Why don't you read it to me?* Be sure to focus on content, not form. If something is not clear, don't hesitate to ask questions of authors. Let them know that you are interested in what they have to say and want to know as much as possible.

You may wish to help your young authors keep a *Writer's Log* of exciting ("juicy") words, wonderful phrases, or figurative language that children are using in their daily writing. Praise the deed and you will see it repeated over and over again! You may also wish to keep—for your private enjoyment—a journal of invented spellings that are simply too good to forget, such as *cow-q-later*.

As children begin finishing stories, you will want to have a mini-lesson on *peer conferences*. Introduce the areas of the room that have been set aside for peer conferences and establish the rules necessary for effective conferences to take place. Review with children the check-off sheet that helps focus the conferences (see page 49). Be sure children know the *purpose* of the conference. Is it a conference that will improve content or one that will focus on editing? Teach them how to help one another make their stories more detailed and better organized. The more modeling you do, the more effective the conferencing will be. You may wish to role-play some good and bad peer conference situations. The following is an example of a mini-lesson done with the class, using an overhead projector and a student's writing sample. The purpose of the mini-lesson was to model how, through questioning, peers can help friends make their stories more detailed. For reproducible forms for peer and editing conferences, see pages 46–50. Duplicate a number of whichever forms are appropriate for children and keep them with your other writing materials. Once you have demonstrated how they are used, children will have no trouble using the forms on their own.

Teri, a first-grade student in a bilingual classroom, gave us permission to ask questions that would help her add more details to her story. Her writing had been placed on transparent film so the whole class could see her work. She took hold of the overhead pen and willingly added details to each page as she was questioned (using a different color marker than she used for the first draft). After Teri modeled this procedure, other children were eager to try questioning one another to see whether they, too, might add more detail to their stories. Children selected pieces of writing and buddied-up to revise their work. This was an easy and pleasant way for first-graders to revisit their writing. Teri's additions are not italicized to distinguish them from her original story.

Horse
by Teri

I asked my mom if I could get on my horse. My mom said yes. She knows I can ride horses.

~

QUESTION ASKED BY ANOTHER STUDENT:

Why did your mom say yes? My mom would never let me ride on a horse!

Then me and my horse went for a walk. I love to walk. We went to take a walk around the block.

~

QUESTION ASKED BY STUDENTS:

Why did you go for a walk? Where did you go?

Then we went home to eat food. My horse eats hay. I like to watch my horse eat. I ate corn and chicken and other things. We had a big dinner.

~

QUESTIONS ASKED
BY STUDENTS:

What are you doing in the picture? What did you eat for dinner?

Then we went home to go to bed. My horse sleeps on the front part, near the fence. I sleep in my bed.

~

QUESTIONS ASKED
BY STUDENTS:

Where does the horse sleep? Where do you sleep?

Kindergarten Content Chart

1. I read my work to my friend. ☐

2. My friend listened and gave me compliments. ☐
☐

My Name _____

My Friend's Name _____

Editing Chart
for Grades 1–2

Title of My Story:

_____

☐   I used my best handwriting.

☐   I used capital letters
        and periods.

☐   I drew pictures that go with
        my story.

☐   I practiced reading my story.

My Name_____

Revision Chart
for Grades 1–2

Title of My Story:

_____

_____

1. My friend asked me
   questions about my story. ☐

2. I added more details to
   my story. ☐

My Name_____

My Friend's Name_____

Content Chart
for Grades 1-2

I will check these with my peer.

Title of My Story:

_____

1. My writing makes sense
    when I read it.   ☐

2. I used my best words to
    make my writing more
    interesting.   ☐

3. My story has a beginning,
    a middle, and an ending.   ☐

My Name_____

My Peer's Name_____

My Editing Checklist

My Name_____

Title of My Story_____

1. All my sentences begin with capital letters. ☐

2. All my sentences end with the correct
punctuation (. ? !). ☐

3. I used interesting words in all my sentences. ☐

4. My sentences do not all begin in the
same way. ☐

5. I checked my spelling to the best of my ability. ☐

- -

My Editing Checklist

My Name_____

Title of My Story_____

1. All my sentences begin with capital letters. ☐

2. All my sentences end with the correct
punctuation (. ? !). ☐

3. I used interesting words in all my sentences. ☐

4. My sentences do not all begin in the
same way. ☐

5. I checked my spelling to the best of my ability. ☐

The next thing you will need to do is to model the behavior you expect of your children during **whole-class sharing** time when children will be sharing first drafts of their stories with their classmates. For your born performers, these will be cherished moments. Shyer children will require some encouragement and patience, however. Be sensitive to those children for whom whole-class sharing is a scary prospect. Properly handled, their first experiences will be such positive ones that they will happily come back for more. Use a role-playing situation to show the effects of positive and negative feedback. Focus on teaching positive comments. Be sure you are always the first person to offer feedback to the sharer whenever whole-class sharing takes place. Children will follow your lead. Encourage them to tell the author one *specific* thing that they liked about his or her piece. For example, "I really liked the way you described your favorite pizza. I could almost taste it!" Or, "You made a pretty picture of your grandma's garden." When children are doing a good job on positive comments, model how to make *suggestions* in a positive way. Encourage children to follow your lead here as well.

After five or six weeks, you are ready to have a mini-lesson on the **selection of a writing piece for publication**. Ask children to sort their writing into three piles:

Pile 1—Throw Away
Pile 2—Not Bad
Pile 3—Great Stuff!

Out of the Great Stuff! pile, children may select one piece to publish. These pieces will be carried through *each* step of the writing process. Up to this point, children may have touched on prewriting, drafting, peer conferencing, and possibly, revision as they worked. However, work selected for publication represents their *best* work and passes through these steps:

1. Teacher conference for content and final editing;
2. Peer conference for editing, using peer's knowledge, child's own knowledge, and resources available in classroom;
3. Word processing;
4. Illustration;
5. Binding with combs or rings.

Introduce the **publishing** area to children in a mini-lesson. Point out the designated area and explain the use of all the materials there. Model the use of each item, using samples of books and stories already published, so children will understand your expectations. Be sure to show them a variety of publications, so they will understand that there are a number of possible formats—all of which are acceptable.

In another mini-lesson, demonstrate to children what a **publishing conference** might look like and show children how you would edit their work. Explain that transparent film will be placed over and clipped to each page of their selected pieces. Children will then use fine-tipped markers to make final revisions and corrections. The use of transparencies helps in rewriting and allows each child's first draft to remain intact. In addition, the use of colorful markers and transparent film makes the rewriting process fun! Having fun is a powerful incentive in the elementary grades.

Once the rewrite process is complete, children's final drafts are ready to be entered into the *computer*. Parent volunteers are invaluable for this task. Have them work from the first draft and transparency combo, rather than having children do a complete rewrite of the final draft. If *radical* changes have been made, help children do cut-and-paste versions before turning the stories over to a parent. If the volunteer typist has any questions, children will be happy to answer them. By the second half of the school year, second-graders can input their own stories with an amazing degree of success. They may even continue to make editorial changes as they type— just as real editors do! Once the stories have been input, they are printed out; placed between blank card-stock covers; bound with plastic combs, metal rings, or brass fasteners; and returned to the students. Children will enjoy illustrating the covers and inside pages.

Whole-class sharing and celebrating takes place once again with published work. Encourage every child who has published a piece to take his or her place in the Author's Chair. Help children realize that their stories are meant to be shared, just like the stories by adult authors that they hear during story time. Shelve the completed masterpieces in the class library right next to all the other library books to be enjoyed during Sustained Silent Reading (SSR) time. Keep in mind that only *published* work is considered a "completed masterpiece." *Published* in this case means examples of children's **best** work that have been taken through each step of the publishing process (see page 52). It would be impossible to publish all their work and it would devalue the process as well. Pieces not published may be kept in their folders or "finished work" envelopes.

Classroom Management

One of the most challenging tasks process writing teachers face is that of classroom management. Because the classroom environment during Writer's Workshop has an enormous effect on children's eagerness to participate, it is important to create a risk-free, positive climate for all. Such a climate can only be achieved when you are focused and well organized. The following topics should be considered as you work toward accomplishing this goal.

✎ Organization and Student Ownership

A writing workshop, like any other workshop for any age group, cannot function well without structure. Organization of materials, space, and children's roles and expectations is critical. It is important to model all facets of the workshop structure and to be sure that student ownership is a built-in part of each facet. Time should be set aside to debrief and problem solve whenever necessary. Helping children make lists of what Writer's Workshop "Looks Like" and "Sounds Like" is a good organizational tool that helps children get back on the right track and allows them to take an important step toward becoming self-directed learners.

Such lists might contain the following child-generated items with rebus pictures.

Looks Like ~
1. Some writers working at their desks.
2. Teacher conferencing with child or students.
3. Some children publishing on the computer.
4. Some writers conferencing in the peer-conferencing corners.
5. Some writers illustrating their published pieces.

6. Some writers looking at the Hot Topics chart to get new ideas.

Sounds Like ~

1. Student writers silently writing.
2. Teacher and child or students using quiet voices during conferences.
3. Children using quiet voices during peer conferences.
4. Children using soft hands to type on the computer.
5. Children using soft feet to move from place to place.

Scheduling

At times, Writer's Workshop may start to self-destruct because teachers neglect to include all the components in the workshop schedule. Some teachers make the mistake of having children write for the entire time. This may work for some children, but it definitely does not always work for all, especially primary students. Off-task behavior may be a direct result. Other teachers may forget to stop for whole-class sharing sessions, thus depriving their students of necessary positive feedback. Be sure that your Writer's Workshop is well balanced with adequate time for all the components.

1. Mini-Lesson—5–10 minutes
2. Writing and Conferencing—20–25 minutes
3. Group Share—5–10 minutes

Status of the Class

Occasionally, process writing teachers get frustrated with the workshop concept because in allowing for individuality, some children may easily become lost in the shuffle. A technique called *status of the class* can help a teacher know what children are working on at all times, in addition to holding children accountable. The teacher simply calls out the name of each child and records where they are in the writing process on a specially prepared chart that contains the names of all children in a vertical column and the days of the week across the top. For example, if a child responds, "I'm making a thinking chart for my birthday story," the teacher simply records the letters *PW* (prewriting) next to the child's name for that day.

Some teachers also find it helpful to include a place for *sharing* and *materials needed* on the "Status of the Class" sheet. For example, if there are five computers available for publishing, only five children at a time can be working at this stage of the process. Listing this under the *materials needed* heading helps organize the workshop. Picking one child to share that day, during "Status of the Class" time, eliminates interruptions from others eager to share. Teacher conferencing can then flow more smoothly. See page 57 for a reproducible format for "Status of the Class."

~ Status of the Class ~

Names	Mon.	Tues.	Wed.	Thurs.	Fri.	Sharing	Materials Needed
						Mon.	
						Tues.	
						Wed.	
						Thurs.	
						Fri.	

Abbreviations for Writing Process:
   Prewriting = PW   Publishing/Computer = P/C   Editing = E
   Conferencing = CP (peer) CT (teacher)   Illustrating = I   Sharing = SH

✎ Signals

Many primary teachers have found it helpful to use signals when organizing Writer's Workshop. The following signals have been used effectively, or you may wish to create your own.

The Silent Writing Signal ~

Primary students may often find it difficult to settle into silent writing. Some teachers draw a star on the chalkboard to signal the start of silent writing. A tagboard star may also be placed in the front of the room by a monitor, or a simple sign that says *silent writing* may be posted. Whichever way you choose, children know it is time to write by themselves. When the star or sign is removed, children may begin peer conferences.

3–2–1 Countdown ~

Use this countdown signal to quickly and quietly move children in and out of the mini-lesson and whole-class sharing areas. When the teacher is holding up three fingers, it means to stand up quietly. Two fingers tell children to face the place they are going to. One finger signals soft feet to walk into or out of the specific area. Children may also be invited to do the countdown in place of the teacher.

✎ Floating Teacher

Teachers of primary writers have found that children stay on task better if the teacher moves around the room rather than holding conferences in just one spot. Placing a small chair next to the desks of children you are conferencing with allows you proximity with more children and provides opportunities for you to model the use of quiet voices. When you are done with one child, simply tote the chair to the next child's desk who is ready for a conference.

Record keeping and Assessment

The development of a system of record keeping that allows you to authentically assess the growth of your children as writers is an important aspect of Writer's Workshop. You need a way to keep track of how well children write, how they have grown as writers, and what skills they have mastered. This section of *Primary Writer's Workshop* contains systems that have been used successfully by primary teachers of process writing. They may be helpful in developing your own personal record-keeping system. Keep in mind that no one system works well for everyone. You may need to pick and choose from the suggestions here to come up with the perfect system for your classroom.

Collect and save student writing.

This system is easily done using the two-folder approach described in the materials section (see page 16). One folder is the *Work in Progress* folder. The other is the *Completed Work Folder* or envelope. Frequent analysis of children's work will enable you to observe their emerging strengths as writers. Be sure, when you conference with children, to add *dated* comments to their writing folders in the areas labeled *strengths* and *skills to practice*. The checklist provides a list of particular skills to consider (see pages 68–69). It is also a good idea to periodically go through the writing folders to match up and check off skills that have been mastered and those that need attention. You may wish to do this right before report cards go out. Staple the checklists to the portfolios to create a year-long running record. You, as well as children and parents, may then begin to celebrate what children *can* do.

Recognize the developmental writing stages of your students and become familiar with the behaviors expected at each stage. ✐ ✐ ✐

Process writing teachers need to recognize and validate the three stages of writing development, so their observations and recordings are targeted appropriately for each child. The stages are described with appropriate examples below.

✎ Emergent Stage

Children who are just beginning to write are at the *emergent* stage. They may draw, scribble-write, or use isolated letters to tell their stories. If letters are used at all, they are usually letters that appear in the children's names or that are taken from environmental print.

I Lost My Cat

One day my cat ran out his little door.

I found him on the next-door neighbor's lawn.

He licked me on the lips. We were happy.

Nicole uses scribble-writing and pictures to tell her story. She has established correct directional movement across the page and has told a complete story.

Batman

Batman talks to Robin. Robin wants to work on the computer.

Robin has his suit off. Robin works on the computer.

This is their computer. Robin stopped the computer. He went to sleep.

Shawn is using initial and ending consonants to tell his story. He has combined scribble-writing with the use of letter sounds. He seems to place his letters and words in random order, but he has told a complete story.

I am real mad because Justin likes Bubba.

Justin likes Bubba. Bubba is mean.

I kicked Bubba and Justin out. My cousin came to play.

April uses words she knows and sounds that letters make to tell a story about her cousin. She has established some directionality (top to bottom, left to right) and shows an awareness of conventional print.

✎ Early Stage

Children at the *early* stage are becoming more aware of how print works and are beginning to make use of invented spelling. Their stories are more developed and their illustrations match the text.

Horse

My horse takes a good night's sleep so she can have a good start in the morning.

I asked my mom if I can take a little ride on my horse and she said yes.

And I fed my horse some hay and after I fed my horse some dinner, I went inside to eat my dinner.

Bianca has written a complete story about her horse. She uses initial, middle, and ending letters in her words. She places vowels correctly in some of her words, although they are not necessarily the correct vowels. She has spacing between her words as well.

***My Book
About Dinosaurs***

***Dinosaurs make
footprints in the
desert.
I have seen them in
a museum.***

***Dinosaurs are little
and big. Some have
spikes and some
have horns. Some
have big tails. They
use their tails to
smack
each other.***

***Dinosaurs eat and
eat and eat plants
and some
dinosaurs eat
meat.***

***Some dinosaurs die
when they fight.***

John has chosen to write about a nonfiction topic. He sticks to his topic
on each page and develops details about dinosaurs. He also shows an
awareness of the need for capital letters and periods.

✎ Fluent Stage

Children at the fluent stage have become independent writers. They write freely with ease and confidence, no longer struggling with writing conventions and letter formation. Both writing and illustrations are well developed.

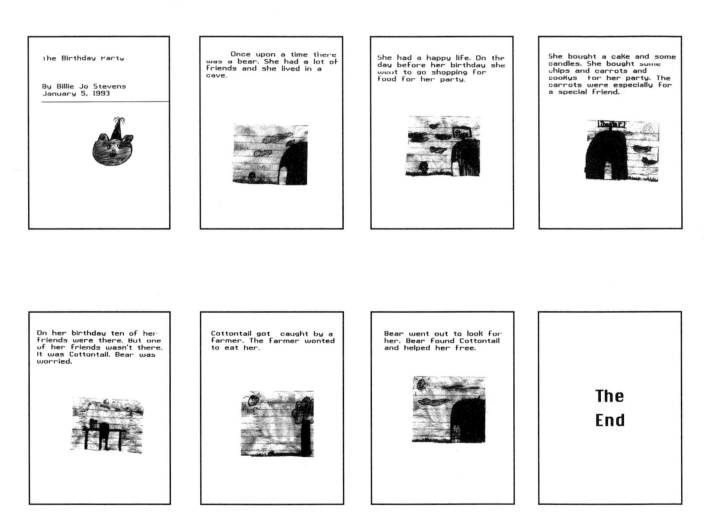

The Birthday Party

By Billie Jo Stevens
January 5, 1993

Once upon a time there was a bear. She had a lot of friends and she lived in a cave.

She had a happy life. On the day before her birthday she went to go shopping for food for her party.

She bought a cake and some candles. She bought some chips and carrots and cookys for her party. The carrots were especially for a special friend.

On her birthday ten of her friends were there. But one of her friends wasn't there. It was Cottontail. Bear was worried.

Cottontail got caught by a farmer. The farmer wonted to eat her.

Bear went out to look for her. Bear found Cottontail and helped her free.

The End

Billy Jo has written a story about a bear that contains a variety of characters. It is logical in both plot development and sequence and demonstrates knowledge of story structure. Billy Jo has used knowledge gained by reading to enhance her character development.

The Cat and Dog and Rat

By: Carol

January 4, 1993

My cat and dog and rat sleep together during the day and night. Then they eat together. They like to play together and sometimes they even sleep on my bed. They cuddle up beside me. They know I will not roll over on them.

1.

I take the dog and the cat and the rat for a walk with my mom and dad in the park. I like to swing my rat on the swing. I nearly hurt my rat George by pushing the swing to fast. It was just a little push.

2.

Later my dog barked and then my cat jumped up onto the swing. I decided to put the dog and the cat and the rat on the same swing. They were on top of each other.

4.

The dog barked and the cat meowed and the rat squeaked! I said,"Oh, no!" "They're going to fall!!"

5.

I ran up to catch them but they didn't fall!!!! I took them off the swing and I took them into the field to play.

I tied the dog's leash to a bar. I gave the cat to my mom. I kept the rat with me because he was still shivering!!!!

7.

I might take them back to the park another day.

MAYBE!!!!!

Carol has developed a story with many details and has even included a bit of humor at the end. She has demonstrated appropriate use of both punctuation and grammar. Carol's writing is enhanced by many juicy words, such as *cuddle*, *squeaked*, and *shiver*.

Record skill development and strengths during conferences and sharing sessions ✏ 🖎 ✎

Make notes on overall growth, mastery of individual skills, confidence as a writer, and awareness of writing as a process for each child. Place your notes on the "writing folder contents" sheets attached to the inside of the writing folders (see page 18)—they can be used later when assessing the child with a developmental writing checklist. Some sample checklists you may wish to use are on pages 68–69. Remember—the best and most effective checklists are those you create because they will reflect the exact skills children are working on in your classroom.

Involve children in keeping track of their progress. ✏ 🖎 ✎

Make use of the forms on pages 68–69 or devise your own to assist children in recognizing what they are doing well in their writing. This is a powerful form of assessment. Once again, it helps you empower children and assists them in setting goals for their own writing. These forms can also be shared by children or teachers during parent conference time. Kindergarten students may be interviewed by teachers and their words recorded on the kindergarten sheet.

Watch Out for Whales!

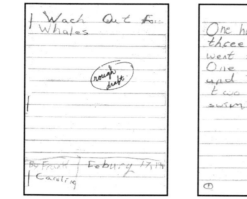

| Wach Out Fo
Whales

(rough draft)

By Frank Febuary 17,14
Caroline

One hot sunny Day
three friends
went to the beach
One was surfing
and the other
two went
swiming.

①

There names
were Frankie
Caroline and Mrs.
Daybon.

②

Frankie fell of
his surfing
board when a
whale captured
us when he
opened his jaws
at the top of
the wave.

③

Then the
whale swaled
us all. We wea
so scared that
the whale started
tickling us

④

We made
a tire out
of sticks and
stones so we
could get out
when he opened
Hemungos jaws.

⑤

Then we flew
out of Hemungos jaw
of the whale
Then we swam
so fast the
went to the
bottom of the sea
7that we got
on land just
like that.

⑥

We lived
Happily even
after And after
that we never
went to sea again

7

Rough draft developed from story structure on page 26.

~ Developmental Writing Checklist ~
Emergent and Early Stage

Name_____	✔ /Date			Comments
Uses pictures to convey messages				
Uses scribble-writing to convey messages				
Uses letters or letter-like forms				
Demonstrates linearity, directionality				
Writes initial consonants				
Writes initial and final consonants				
Writes some middle letters in words				
Uses spaces between words				
Writes some whole words				
Writes simple sentences that make sense				
Developing sense of beginning, middle, and end				
Sequences ideas logically				
Matches illustrations to text				
Able to read own writing				
Beginning to use capitals and periods				

~ Developmental Writing Checklist ~
Fluent Stage

Name_____	✔ /Date				Comments
Confidently chooses topics					
Organizes ideas logically					
Uses supporting details					
Fully develops beginning, middle, and ending					
Uses varied sentence lengths					
Varies sentence beginnings					
Increases fluency (writing longer pieces)					
Writes in a variety of styles: Personal Expression Narrative Story Informative Persuasive					
Willing to revise work					
Uses punctuation marks and capitalization more accurately					
Uses resources to check spelling					
Willingly shares writing					

Name_____ **Date**_____

I Am A Writer!

_____

_____

_____

_____

_____

_____

_____

_____

_____

_____

Gr. K

Name_____ **Date**_____

Look What I Can Do...

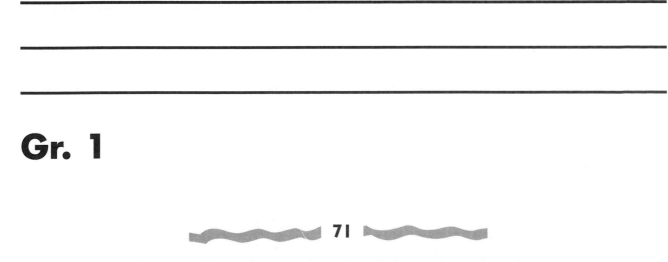

I can_____

_____

_____

_____

_____

I still need to work on_____

_____

_____

_____

_____

Gr. 1

Name_____ **Date**_____

My Writing Is Improving Because...

I can _____

_____

_____

_____

_____

_____

I will make it even better by

_____

_____

_____

_____

Gr. 2

Parent Connection

Communicate with Parents

Keep in mind the importance of communicating with parents when you institute something like Writer's Workshop in your classroom, so they have a clear understanding of your plans and goals. Process writing may be confusing and even upsetting to parents who have never been exposed to invented or temporary spelling. It is possible that they may regard a young child's first writings as sloppy, misspelled scribbling that should never have been sent home. They may even be critical—a situation worth avoiding at all cost.

Educate Parents

Parents need to be made aware of what is involved in Writer's Workshop— the importance of the process and how it works. *Process* is the key word. In these days of instantaneous microwaved, computerized, or remote-controlled gratification, the idea of *process* has become somewhat foreign. But there is still a place in life—many places—for the idea of reworking, refining, and plain old practicing.

It is equally important for parents to understand the important role process writing plays in reading. Parents who are knowledgeable about the reading-writing connection are bound to be enthusiastic and supportive— at home as well as in school. Consider using examples of student work to explain Writer's Workshop at your Back-to-School Night or sending home a newsletter in the fall explaining the program. The checklist on page 76 is helpful in promoting family understanding and involvement.

If you are using authentic assessment—and process writing lends itself naturally to this form of assessment—you are able to show parents the progress their children are making in a concrete way by collecting samples of children's writing over time. Be sure to inform parents of their children's growth in writing, in their use of skills, and in their attitude toward writing at your regularly scheduled parent-teacher conferences. Sharing writing samples collected throughout the year provides important tangible evidence of growth for parents.

Invite Parent Participation

School budgets being what they are, it makes sense to capitalize on parent power whenever you can. Families who become actively involved in school projects become wonderful sources of positive PR. With your help and perhaps a few hours of after-school training, parents can become involved in conferencing, editing, publishing, and illustrating. Kindergarten and first-grade teachers find parents invaluable for computer inputting of student books. Some schools have even set up Print Shops run entirely by parents. Children come to the Print Shop when they are ready to publish, design covers, or illustrate the pages. Consider sending home the letter on page 75 to request parent volunteers.

Dear Family:

Our young writers need you! Please try to attend an informal informational meeting about Writer's Workshop in our classroom on _____ at _____ . There are lots of ways you can help. We hope you'll be able to come lend a hand.

Thank you for your interest and support for our writing program.

Sincerely,

_____

- -

Student Name_____

Parent/Guardian_____

Please check the appropriate box and return to school by_____.

❏ I would like to help with the Writer's Workshop program and I will attend the meeting.

❏ I cannot attend the meeting but I'd like to help if I can. Please call me at _____ and tell me more.

❏ I am unable to help at this time.

Parent Checklist

How to Help My Child as a Writer

I will model writing myself.

I will supply materials and encourage my child to write
(paper of all sizes, pencils, chalk, crayons, markers).

I will help my child spell words by listening for the letters we hear.
For example, house = *h-u-s*, blue = *b-l-u*.

I will encourage my child to write:

- shopping lists
- recipes
- thank-you notes
- letters
- stories
- little books

I will encourage my child to use family experiences for writing topics.

- outings
- holidays
- special events

I will listen and compliment my child when he or she reads his or her writing. For example, "I like the way you told the whole story!"

Finally, here are a few tips for the Writer's Workshop teacher.

1. Take advantage of every teachable moment. It is important to keep Writer's Workshop as child-centered as possible. When the instruction emerges from the children's needs, it becomes instantly relevant and meaningful.

2. Maintain a sense of joy in the process. The creation of a writing environment for young children is a gift you give them. Share their delight in the gift.

3. Introduce skills, such as the use of exclamation marks or quotation marks, as they occur naturally in children's writings. Suddenly everyone will be using them!

4. Be flexible in your planning, scheduling, and conferences. If you try to adhere too rigidly to a system or schedule, you'll wind up feeling frustrated. In the primary grades, flexibility is crucial. A sense of humor doesn't hurt either!

5. *Celebrate* every sign of growth, no matter how small. Share it with everyone, because the enthusiasm created by successes in Writer's Workshop is very contagious!

Good luck!

References

Janine Batzle, *Portfolio Assessment and Evaluation* (Creative Teaching Press, 1992).

Lucy M. Calkins, *The Art of Teaching Writing* (Heinemann, 1986).

Donald Graves, *Writing: Teachers and Children at Work* (Heinemann, 1983).

Linda Karges-Bone and Veronica Terrill, *Primarily Portfolios* (Good Apple, 1995).

Regie Routman, *Invitations* (Heinemann, 1991).

Teacher Notes

Teacher Notes